Survival Communication:

20 Communicative Skills To Stay In Touch With Your Family When the World Goes Silent

Table of content

Introduction

Nowadays, it is difficult to imagine a life without modern technology, but you have to learn how to live without these things. After a disaster, the world goes silent because the networks and advanced technology may not work. After a catastrophe, hurricane or any other catastrophe, you have to find out your lost family members. You should have an alternative to a cell phone for emergency communication. It is difficult to predict the actual time of any disaster, and these sudden events can destroy everything in your life.

To make your life easy and reduce the damage during these events, you should focus on the advance planning. Try to buy all necessary devices and tools that can be used as a natural alternative to the cell phone. You can buy a CB radio for easy communication and satellite phones. You can get the advantage of different types of devices and tools available to you. It will be good to investigate about available devices and get some devices for your family members.

You can set a particular point of meeting with your family members to gather there after a disaster. Train them how to behave in an emergency situation. It will prove helpful for you to increase the protection of your family members. In this book, you will learn different methods of communication after the world goes silent.

Chapter 1 – Radio as a source of communication

Disaster is a natural calamity that can inflict anyone anywhere at any time. They can be in the form of hurricane, tornado, and earthquake. In the setting of this modern era of high technology and automation, nuclear wars, terrorist charge or EMP (Electro Magnetic Pulse) strike are also disastrous conditions. They result in a great deal of destruction in terms of life, money or property. These disasters not only come with destruction but means of communication are also riled.

Every latest amenity provided to humans so far is lost. There s no food, electricity or means of communication. All the ways to inform someone or any organization, about the situation of a place or person, is severed. There is no setup of phone calls, text messages or internet connection.

These disasters don't come with a warning, but when inflicted there is no way out. They don't give you the chance to re-think or repeat what has already occurred. As prevention is better than cure so, you should compose yourself as you have to cope up this battle alone.

Reliable means of communication are as inevitable as are the troops, guns, radar or food is. As these are the mean to survival but the facility to communicate could be a bridge to survival and the ability to inform concerned authorities of your ruinous condition can help you escape this atrocity.

Below are some means of communication which can be helpful in disastrous a predicament that can help you to cope up with the situation and save your and others life with limited resources in hand.

1. CB Radios:

Citizens Band Radio or pronounced short as CB radio are dated back to its first use in the 1940s. With 40 channels selection, they have a range of 27 MHz (11 m) band. Unlike other radios, possession of CB radio does not require a license in many countries and are for business and personal use. They are more frequently used than other radios. Due to its availability, they can be quite helpful in disaster condition, but they do possess many limitations which confine its use.

A lot of people have CB radio but not all of them. Its main disadvantage does not come with its availability but number of people using it in the approachable range as your CB radio's range. CB radios also require long aerial and has poor propagation signal indoor limiting its use.

The greatest reason of the failure of CB radios range comes from its power which is 5-watt input with 4-watt out declining its advantage over other systems. The range of CB radio can be increased if they are given more power. With this frequency, they cover 1 to 10 miles. Their coverage area can be increased if they are boosted with an amplifier. Many people do have CB radio at the same time but if they are not using it at the same time, so you cannot communicate with them.

Illegally, the range of CB radio is increased by some people by use of transmitters which do increase its range to hundreds of miles but it produces a problem with its short range of signals which are difficult to hear than long distance signals. Increasing its range is amenable to punishment by FCC (Federal Communication Commission). But increasing range so that you can hear and contact farther is of no use if the person, on the other hand has CB radio with a normal transmission.

2. The Spark Gap Transmitter:

The spark gap transmitters were first used in 1800 and literally the first device to be used for radio transmission. These transmitters work by generating spark across a spark gap in the transmitter. Their advantage is that they are easily manufactured and are easily used. They have a huge range working over a number of frequencies and also as a back-up for distress messages on the international distress frequency of 500 kHz (600 meters) right up to the beginning of World War II.

The thing make its use is illegal, is its range. Also transmission of signals and understanding them require expertise as the messages transmitted can only be understood if the person knows the Morse code or they have their own transmission code to interpret what is being said.

3. Crystal Radios

Crystal radio receiver or a crystal set or cat's whisker receiver was first used in early the 20th century. They are the simplest radio receiver that can be easily made at household items like some wires, antenna, capacitor, crystal detector and earphones. It receives its power by power of radio waves which is received by its antennas no external power source is required for them to work, quite easy to use. They derive their name of crystal radio because of Galena, a crystal mineral used as crystal detector.

4. The Foxhole Radio:

The foxhole radio dated back to WWII, when they were first use. They are also simple to make, using a razor blade as radio wave detector. They don't require external power source but derive its power from the signals they receive. They can only receive signals but can't transmit.

5. Repeaters:

A repeater is a device which can transmit signals repeatedly to increase its power so it could be heard at a longer distance as during transmission much power is lost in term of heat or electric current. A repeater consists of a radio receiver, an amplifier, a transmitter, an isolator, and two antennas. They omit the nuisance during a transmission making signals and sound clear. There are a lot of people around the corner using repeaters as a mean of communication. They carry signals from radios in its surrounding and increase its power to be heard at a longer distance. People who use repeaters are on emergency communication and keep backup power as they use an external source of power.

The internet does have repeaters. All you need is to click repeater option and have to write the address of another person using a repeater and what you will be saying over your radio can be heard on the other side of the hand.

6. GMRS/FRS/MURS radios:

GMRS, FRS and MURS are abbreviations of General Mobile Radio Service, Family Radio Service and Multi-Use Radio Service respectively. Much of the CB radios now have been replaced by GMRS/FRS/MURS radios. They are cheap and easy to use. They are used by a number of individuals and businesses companies. FRS and MURS do not require licensing by FCC but GMRS frequencies do require licensing by FCC. Their use is limited because of its power and shorter range coverage.

If a GMRS is connected to a repeater, it can increase its range and can cover hundreds of miles but it needs a repeater to be working properly and you should be in the range of repeater for the reception of the signals. GMRS were formerly called as "Class A CB". It has the advantage over many other radios that it can be used at higher power. The best selection among these radios could be a GMRS for which you need an FCC license.

7. Amateur radio (ham radio):

The Amateur radios were first used in late 19th century or early 20th century. They are used for non-commercial messages, memo or information transmission by use radio frequency spectrum. Messages can be sent in the form of voice, images and other modes of data. Their range of transmission varies from 10 meters to 2000 meters. Their range of frequencies is called "band plan" and are assigned by local bodies and foreign treaty or between Amateur radio operators. Because of its broad telecommunication range, it is the first choice for emergency or disaster conditions, even used by what MARS (the Military Auxiliary Radio System), ARES (Amateur Radio Emergency Service), emergency, rescue and search teams.

The national weather system (NOAA) frequencies can be stationed in amateur radios through which you can acquire the idea of what is going on in your area. If a radio scanner is lodged in it, you can reach emergency frequencies, getting know-how of emergency situations, without knowing which frequency they are broadcasting. It scans by automatically tuning or scanning different frequencies and stopping where it finds reception and then continues to scan if the first transmission ceases.

Chapter 2 – HACKS TO USE PHONE AS A   SOURCE OF COMMUNICATION

Our whole lives are revolving around high tech technologies with which we have conquered the world. One of such technology is the mobile phone. Mobile phones have squeezed the distances among people. When a disaster hits a place or country not only homes, building or roads are destroyed, but the entire infrastructure is ruined. As mobile phone networking is based on such a vast infrastructure, it too gets affected in a disastrous situation. In this condition, when you don't have the facility to call or text someone for help then Satellite phones could be the best option to go for with which you can not only communicate friends or family members but also to the rescue teams.

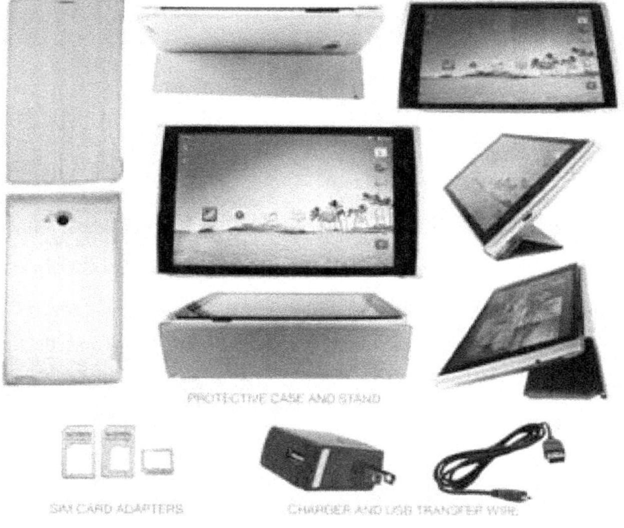

Satellite phones or sat phones just work like mobile phone except that they don't need terrestrial infrastructure for communication but connect to roaming satellite in the space for signal transmission. Calls, text messages or even low bandwidth internet can be used via it. Depending upon the construction, they can cover a small area of a land or the whole globe.

All rescue and search teams are equipped with satellite phones so they can reach other local or international rescue teams or hospitals or authorities at the time of need without relying on mobile phone services.

For an entrepreneur, it is necessary for them to get them equipped with satellite phone as a part of disaster management program. This is not only for the safety of themselves as well as their employees.

Initially, satellite phones were of big sizes, but now they have been compacted to the size of the latest smartphones. Satellite phones are also being marked with being expensive but with advancement, they are being modernized to low affordable cost. Its cost varies with the services provided with each handset like internet access.

Emergency preparation

8) We all have been aware of landline service since very early time, but there are newer versions which are being operated via electricity. What if you have been inflicted with a disaster; then this landline service is of no use. To overcome this shortcoming, scientists have designed a newer technolo-

gy named as Voice over IP (VoIP), which does not require typical copper made landline wires but work via the internet or broadband connection leaving behind older landline service.

9) If you have a backup plan of latest phone services that run on batteries, keep on checking them, estimate it for how long they can run, learn how to change them, try to save its power to be used in need, keep extra batteries. Try to keep rechargeable batteries, so you do not need to run for them at the end. If you have run out of batteries, buy them and keep some of it in extra quantity and ask nearby providers if they can provide it to you timely.

10) In the case of electricity failure, try to use the phone (that uses electricity as the power supply) less. Disconnect the battery if the phone is not in use and re-connect battery when you need to make or receive an important call. Try to save as much battery as you can. Once the electricity is restored, immediately charge the batteries.

11) If you have landline phone service that needs connection via wires, they can work in power failures, but many cordless home phones rely on electric power to work.

12) Charge your mobile phones, wireless phones if there is any prediction of any calamity to occur. Keep extra batteries and car charger in hand.

13) Charge your laptop, tablets in the case for any emergency. If a blackout occurs and WiFi service is in the vicinity, you can get your laptop or tablet connected and sends emails or can even make voice calls or video calls to call for help. By this, you can not only inform friends or family but can also inform rescue and disaster management teams. In addition, mobile phones can be charged from laptop or tablet to make important calls but be careful, not to consume the whole power of laptop or tablet, in case if you need to go online on laptop or tablet to get connected online.

14) Keep solar powered operated, battery operated or hand crank operated radio or portable television so that they could be used in an emergency situation during dim out. These portable devices can come in handy to have news from broadcasters or news channels that can provide you significant enlighten about the weather forecast, emergency services and where to navigate to safety. For operating these portable equipments, keep extra batteries and take a look at instruction handbook so that you can use them without difficulty in the time of need.

How mobile phones can come in handy in crisis?

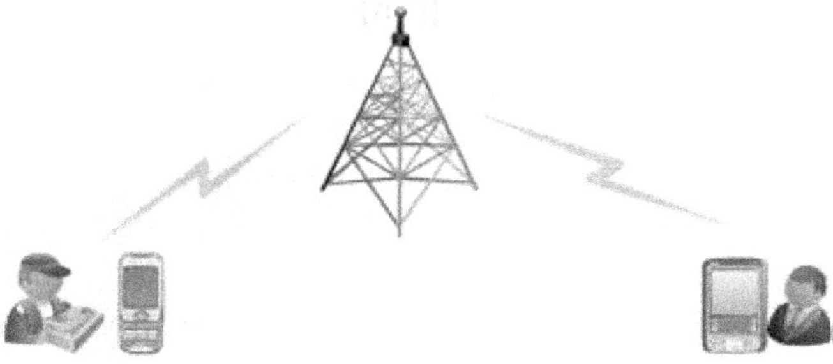

1. Keep your contact list up to date. Store useful contact numbers whom you want to get connected in an emergency situation. Also keep contact numbers of your local police, fire department, disaster management department and utility companies. By keeping all these contacts in hand, you can immediately report concern authorities about power failures, emergency situation, and condition of places affected by a disaster.

2. Assign some contact numbers the emergency contacts. You can even make a group or list entitled as emergency group. By using this group, you can send a single text to a number of concerned contacts so that they can get acquainted with your current situation and location. Some social networking sites are also provided with this service of emergency group formation. By using this service, you can quickly go online and share your status with that group, which would instantly be looked by a number of people who can help you out or inform concerned authorities about the situation.

3. Twitter in the case of emergency- We all are very much aware of Twitter and this number 40404. It's Twitter's text message number. Twitter is becoming an important platform before, during and after a disaster. Many of you are unaware of this fact that you do not need to have a Twitter account for acquiring latest update. You can acquaint with any news or emergency situation via Twitter just by utilizing your phone's text messaging facility (standard text message rates apply).

Everyone should stay connected with a number of official accounts of the local or state level of the emergency department, resource department and disaster management department to be timely informed about any relevant news or information so that useful and appropriate initiative can be taken.

4. Bookmark useful mobile sites- Using an internet connection or cellular data you can easily bookmark those sites which are designed to display important and relevant information about an emergency situation.

5. Reinforce your batteries- Keep some charged batteries or solar-assisted charging devices with which you can recharge your phone in case of any emergency situation without using electricity power source. This can be useful if there is electricity failure for prolonged duration of time.

These initiatives which have been given above can play a crucial role in your survival and help you cope up with the catastrophic situation.

Chapter 3 – HACKS FOR UNCOMMON COMMUNICATION

Disaster management plans are always the key to survival in such atrocity. Preparedness plans are not for a single person but whole families, school children, company's employees and all the individuals in a community. The most distressful situation is faced when people are being forced to face such crisis without their spouse and their children. These plans are designed to lessen life loss and damages. It also reduces their susceptibility to disasters and strengthens their capacities to confront them. These programs are crucial and need to be clearly defined, practiced and initiated in due time without any delay because there is no chance of failure in these plans. These plans include preparing an emergency kit, planning and practicing exit routes, keeping maps or GPS system in hands so they could be used at the time of need. Preparedness plans also include dropping distinctive messages to your family or friends so that they can get aware of your situation in such a crisis.

We are so much familiar with the modern technology that we have completely laid our lives over these inventions, and we have so much gotten used to it that cannot think of our lives without it. Sending text messages and calling loved one's to know about their whereabouts is the very common practice now a day's which can be done within seconds just by a tap or a click but all of it gets off if power supply network shuts down. Although these modern communicating devices have made our lives so much convenient but we cannot completely count on these for our survival especially during a disaster ambience.

When 9/11, Hurricane Katrina, Hurricane Sandy or any other disaster occurred; it not only affected infrastructure but a lot of families got affected which led to the separation of a number of family members. Despite advancement in telecommunication, people were unaided and unable to contact their loved ones and got to know about their locality. Natives were only left with the option of finding their loved ones by posting photographs at Red Cross and FEMA stations and waited for the safe return of their loved ones. We could have been saved with our families if we would have been in our homes with our loved ones, being protected during a disaster bash, but all of this is fiction.

Terrorist attack in Georgia, America would have been ended in seizing all the power supply of America in a terror attack, but due to peerless and competent strategies of FBI, this attack was withheld. These troopers were arrested while attempting to buy pipe bombs and thermite for explosions. These terrorists had made the plan to seize the power grids and water treatment plans leading to the complete shutdown in America and resulting in an energy crisis, all of this was revealed by federal agents in a court hearing. This terror plot would have been accomplished if one of the militants had not been arrested while trying to buy pipe bombs and thermite from an undercover agent. Thermite grenades are one of the deadliest military-grade weapons used by militaries during attacks or defense. They cause destruction over a wide area in terms of life, property or equipment. There had been reports about northern Georgian militant planning out to strike federal government agencies in order to aggravate riots and establish the need for martial law order.

15. Cloth Flags Used as Warning Signs:

The cheapest and easiest method to give signals to rescue teams about your location or situation is by using cloth flags made out of table clothes, curtains or any other clothes. It's a non-verbal, non-written, inexpensive and convenient. For the purpose of signal perception, use more than one spots of your home which should be known by every member of the family where the messages can be found. More than one spots are better because during a crisis there could be a loss of part or property like in a hurricane, storm and fire or restrict movement of a person coming after you when you have already left. As well as assign color code that which color defines safety or evacuation and which assign danger. Assign a particular color or pattern or size to a specific family member so that at the time of crisis the particular person can be located. Assign a specific spot to a specific person of the family, where they can tie their specific cloth, so their status of evacuation can timely be noted without wasting time.

In a disaster, when family members try to evacuate as soon as possible but parents, in spite of danger never leave the place until they get the knowledge about all their off springs have been safely rescued. But in case a child is out to play, in such a situation parents rush out in search of their missing child risking their lives and of the other children as well. A specific colored cloth thread could be the signal of exit route, safety evacuation or meeting place, etc. The message thread should be design which is easy to plan, easy to remember and easy to follow. The escape path can be specified by cloth tie highlighting the route so the family members who have lost their ways due to fright or changed its ways can rejoin other family members at a particular spot which should be devised properly.

16. Survival Graffiti

Art can be life-saving in case of a disaster. Only a spray paint can give a clue about the route of the exit of a person or family who can later be rescued. Family members can be taught about different signals or signs distinct to a particular condition and understood by only specific family members. These practices can be made friendly and joyful as well can be fed in memory of every family member if planned as a game adventure. Not only sign and signals can help to trace but also writing text message directly that "I went to that place, or that way" can be used but these direct clues could alert an unknown person who should not get aware of the location.

The most appropriate way are signs and symbols only known by family members should be used. There could be a possible situation when a wife does not reach home on time, and there is no way to contact. Husband can trace her by following her regular or alternate route to the home where a private message in terms of sign or signal can be found and can reunite the couple without wasting time in unavailing search and suffering others.

17. Emergency Caches

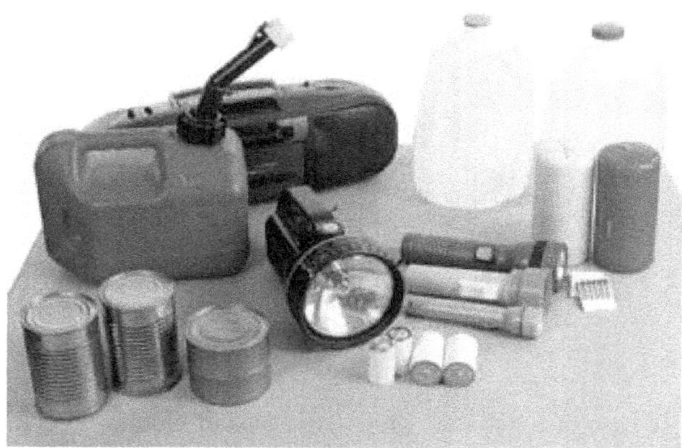

Caches are the substances which are same in type and are stored in unreachable places. Different types of caches can be located at various places only known by family members as trace. These can be placed from school to home or workplace to home at every possible path. These not only provide a trace of the path but also play a role as hidden message and meeting point to reunite. The path of cache needs to skillfully plan out even if it's of short distance covering few miles so that in the case of emergency it can easily be followed.

Hidden messages can be given by placing them in the caches that could be in the form of a pen, paper, painted cans, symbols or simply written message. These messages can serve to re-locate family members, change of plan or meeting point. Any information about personal location can bring about a mental and emotional relief to family members who get separated in any sort of atrocity. The maps about the track of caches should be placed bags, get me home bags, and especially in the children's backpacks and children should be known to these places and those should be approachable at the time of need. In case if the caches are being lost or hidden by a delinquent so there should be emergency caches. These emergency caches serve as ultimate approach retrieve communication and uniting family members once they have been separated.

Chapter 4 – How to Prepare Your House for Blackout Communication?

Disaster either occurring naturally or man made not only affect people but also affect properties. Due to the destruction of the infrastructure not only communication facilities are cut off but also electricity failure occurs that result in black out in the disaster inflicted area. Electricity failure not only affects household or commercial areas but also it destroys water management leading to more difficulties. Advance management in such condition can help you cope up this situation.

Ways to prepare at home in case of power shutdown:

In a case of power loss, traditional land lines and cordless phone which require to be charged get fail. In this condition, when you have already lost power, chargeable phones can never be on your hit list. FCC and FEMA both recommend keeping an old fashioned cord phone, which does not need to get charged, unlike cordless phones. These phones will not run out of battery and can be used if power outages.

16. Car phone chargers are the portable devices carried by mobile phone users in their cars where they can use it to charge their mobile by consuming car's energy. In power shut keep car phone charger for charging your phone when in need and also keep extra charged battery if your mobile battery drain out.

17. Keep an NOAA (National Ocean and Atmospheric) Weather Radio commonly known as NWR should be present. These radios use energy from batteries but can be manually charged by using the hand crank. They can be equipped with a mobile charging outlet as well as flashlights. NWR is a network of radio station spread nationwide, and they continuously broadcast weather information, weather forecast and hazard 24 hours a day and 7 days a week. In collaboration with FCC, NWR gives the accurate weather condition.

19. Upgrade your contact list with one or more than one contact enlisted as ICE. ICE stand for In Case of Emergency. Whenever in a case of emergency when you are unconscious or unable to use the phone, rescue team can search your contact list and can contact your ICE contact but make sure that contact knows that he has been assigned as an ICE contact by you.

20. Follow official government sites and turn on text alerts from state. Twitter is providing this service by sending alert messages during an emergency.

How to communicate effectively during power shutdown?

18. Voice networks are more crowded in an emergency situation than data based services, so FCC and FEMA recommend using text messages, e-mails or social media for non-emergency situations.

19. Try to conserve battery of your mobile so that it can be used for longer periods. Do this by lowering the brightness of your phone as well as turning off those applications which you are not using.

20. If you charge your mobile in your car make sure it's not in the garage and engine is not working

Always try to keep extra batteries so, if you run out of power, there could be a backup power. Check your extra batteries every time and replace them with a new one if they run out of power because batteries are of no use when they run out of power.

These are the hacks when followed can save lives.

Conclusion

After a disaster, you may find it difficult to stay in touch with your family members. This book can solve your problem because you can learn a number of methods for communication. There are lots of items that you can use in the absence of the traditional network.

You should plan everything in advance and get rid of tensions after a disaster. This book can be a real assistance for you. Train your family members to learn the use of these tools and devices. You should keep extra batteries with you and stay connected with each other.

You should teach them how to stay calm after a disaster because anxiety and hurriedness will increase chances of danger. You are responsible for protecting you and your family. You shouldn't forget pets because they are also important.

FREE Bonus Reminder

If you have not grabbed it yet, please go ahead and download your special bonus E book *"Chakras for Beginners. 7 Steps To Understand And Balance Chakras, Radiate Energy, And Strengthen Aura"*.

Simply Click the Button Below

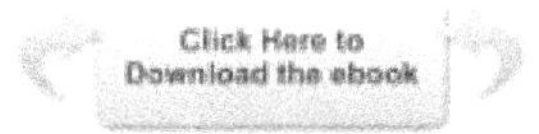

OR Go to This Page

http://lifehacksworld.com/free

BONUS #2: More Free & Discounted Books & Products

Do you want to receive more Free/Discounted Books or Products?

We have a mailing list where we send out our new Books or Products when they go free or with a discount on Amazon. Click on the link below to sign up for Free & Discount Book & Product Promotions.

=> Sign Up for Free & Discount Book & Product Promotions <=

OR Go to this URL

http://zbit.ly/1WBb1Ek